Newbie Pitfalls:
50 Obstacles to Success as a Professional Organizer and How to Avoid Them

By Debbie Stanley

Copyright © Red Letter Day

Revised edition 2020 | 1st ed 2004

ISBN 9780985276836

Contents

Introduction

Introduction

"If I'd only known then what I know now. . . ."

Every veteran professional organizer or productivity consultant (PO/PC) has had that thought at least once. If you're just getting started in your organizing business, you're probably wondering, "What could go wrong and how can I prevent it?"

It's true that lots of things could go wrong—but don't let that scare you away! The professional organizing and productivity field is growing like never before, both in recognition by the public and in resources within the industry for learning from and networking with fellow PO/PCs and related professionals. We built the road for you over the last few decades; now you can walk it with relative ease and, at the same time, blaze your own unique trail.

If you've got the three basic skill sets—being organized, teaching organization, and running a business—your chances for success are very good. If you're working for an organizing firm, you can skip the third item and have one less thing to worry about.

Most PO/PC companies are one-person operations, though, so much of the advice in this book is geared toward those of us who are trying to do it all: Working with clients and functioning as business owners (and trying to prevent those functions from conflicting), all while keeping up with family responsibilities and tending to our own needs as well.

With that much to do, the last thing you need is an obstacle to slow you down, right? Right! So check out the tips, cautions, and hindsight stories in this book, and be ready to dodge those pitfalls before they trip you up.

Please note: The information contained in this book is based on my experiences and opinions, which might differ from yours. My goal is to get you thinking and help you head off trouble before it happens, not to give you the one-and-only way to do things. Most problems have more than one solution, so the solutions you'll find here might fit your needs, or perhaps not. As you read, I urge you to take what's right for you and disregard the rest.

Here's to your successful PO/PC career!

Deb Stanley, Sep 2020

1/50   Letting Fear of Failure Stop You

I chose this pitfall to start with so that we can begin at the logical beginning.

If you're a professional organizing/productivity consulting "newbie"—that's my li'l term of endearment for you—you've probably got some sort of nervousness, anxiety, hesitation, uncertainty, or outright fear about whether this endeavor is going to work. Rest easy, new PO/PC: We've all been where you are.

When I started my company, I kept my "day job" with a publishing firm for three years, working with organizing clients in the evening. I switched to full-time self-employment at that point and took some freelance editorial assignments while I continued to build my organizing client base. Since then, I've focused on client work and organizing-related speaking and writing, but if business gets slow, I can always pick up another freelance editing project.

When I quit my traditional job, a friend called me a risk-taker. He said most people aren't brave or foolish enough to give up a "safe" job and take a shot at self-employment.

Here's what I told him:

> *Look at it this way. If I have a job in a regular company and my boss fires me, I'm unemployed. But if I own my own business and have 20 clients at a time, that means 20 people would have to fire me all at once for me to be truly jobless. And if that happened, I would*

get up the next morning, make my networking rounds, and find more new clients. Now tell me again, which is riskier?

You can succeed at this if you take measured risks, do everything you need to do to make yourself valuable to your clients, and most important, keep trying. If a marketing campaign or particular social media post or membership in some group doesn't pay off, try something else.

You are now, finally, the boss of you.

Bottom Line: It's not failure until you quit trying.

2/50   Being Unprepared for Rapid Growth

When you're new, you tend to spend a lot of time worrying about what you'll do if you don't get enough clients, and no time worrying about what will happen if you get too many at once. You might even think it'd be kind of cool to have people clamoring to hire you.

In truth, it's extremely frustrating to see opportunities passing you by because you weren't ready for your business to grow quite so fast. Set aside what you thought was the worst-case scenario for a minute (yes, you will have clients, don't worry) and think in the opposite extreme.

Suppose you got a mention from a Twitter influencer and 50 people reached out that day to hire you. Is there any way you could accommodate them all at once? How would you choose which of them to work with first? Would you refer some to another PO/PC, and if so, would you ask for a referral fee? How much?

Here are some options, in order of complexity of implementation:

- Hire one or more people to be staff PO/PCs with your company.
- Subcontract PO/PCs to work with clients.
- Refer overflow clients to other PO/PCs and charge a referral fee.
- Share referrals with no exchange of money—just quid pro quo.

Each of these methods has advantages and challenges.

Having PO/PCs on staff means you can train them to work exactly the way you want them to, and you have maximum control over their schedules, but it requires the added task of payroll and tax withholding, plus you'll have to have enough work to keep another person busy.

Subcontracting gets you out of much of the bookkeeping tangle and prevents you from having to provide a consistent amount of work, but it limits how much training you can do and how much control you'll retain over the client/contractor interaction. (Visit the IRS website to research the difference between employees and subcontractors. Search on "Employees vs. Independent Contractors.")

Offering referrals for a fee is simple, but there is still money to be tracked, and you have to be able to trust that the peers who receive your referrals will be honest and send you your cut.

The final option is the easiest: If other PO/PCs send extra business to you as often as you send it to them, everyone can stay busy. However, this option doesn't get you any direct compensation for overflow clients.

No matter how you handle it, one thing is certain: If you get too busy too fast, you will disappoint some new clients and lose them forever.

Bottom Line: Prepare your business for times when there is more work than you yourself can handle so you won't have to miss out on it completely.

3/50   Expecting to Get Rich

With a few notable exceptions, organizing and productivity is not an industry in which you're going to become fabulously wealthy. If you're ambitious and strategic, you can make a comfortable living at it, and that's a great goal. For most people, being able to quit working for someone else and become fully self-employed provides plenty of satisfaction—no need for a mansion and a yacht!

However, some people do go into business with money-making as their top priority. There are plenty of reasons for this (the mortgage, the second mortgage, the car payment, the tuition bill . . .) and it doesn't mean you're greedy if you've got your money on your mind more than most others. Just be aware of a few points:

Go above and beyond

If you want to earn more than most PO/PCs, you'll need to do things that most PO/PCs do not do. This often means close, proactive interaction with the media, especially television, and lots of public speaking and even book-writing.

Embrace the spotlight

In order to become a media favorite, get on TV, get lots of speaking engagements, and become a published author, you will need to know a *lot* about public relations and marketing, not just organizing. If this is your goal, study up!

Keep clients' needs primary

When you're focused primarily on making money, it's very

easy to inadvertently neglect your clients' needs. If your reality is that you need and/or want to earn a lot in this field, then by all means, go for it! But please, for the sake of kindness, choose a specialty that is less likely to bring you into close contact with clients' raw emotions.

If high revenue is your goal, media coverage will be a key marketing tool, and in our industry that means visuals. When reporters want to record you working with your clients, bringing a crew along to a storage unit is much less intrusive than giving them access to a client who is ashamed of the condition of their home. Providing imagery for demonstration of your work can be lovely and impactful, but too often the process devolves into distasteful, disrespectful voyeurism.

Don't think that it's always okay to bring cameras into clients' spaces if you receive permission first. Many clients want very much to earn the approval of their PO/PC, so they will often say yes just to please you. Don't exploit that. If you want to use access to clients' spaces as part of your marketing strategy, you'll need to tread very carefully to stay within ethical boundaries.

Bottom Line: Don't simply expect to get rich. If that's what you want, take the extra steps it requires. Just don't step on clients along the way.

4/50   Dictating to Clients

Here's a really dangerous one: Telling clients what to do.

"But, Deb," you might be thinking, "if we don't tell them what to do, how will anything get done?"

Certainly you will advise clients, guide their decisions, reinforce what they're doing effectively, and try to steer them away from things you know won't work. But you can do all of this and more without actually telling them what to do. There are two reasons this is especially important:

1. If you make decisions for your clients, they will not learn to make decisions for themselves. The improvements you implement will last longer if clients have a role in making the decisions that go into them. Get them involved in deciding where to store categories of items, what types of containers to use, what names to give to file folders, etc. Make suggestions, even tell them what you think will work best, but also tell them why, and empower them to make the final decision.

2. If you take responsibility for clients' decisions, they can sue you for those decisions. Never, ever, ever force a client to get rid of an item. You must make it very clear that decisions on discarding belongings or destroying documents are the sole responsibility of the client, and your advice and behavior must back that up. This is true even of those clients who tell us, "I want you to be firm with me—make me get rid of stuff!"

The most significant thing I've seen a client discard was her mother's wedding dress. I didn't directly tell her to do it, but it was because of her work with me that she was able to make the decision.

We found the dress in a closet, partially wrapped in tissue inside an unsealed cardboard box. I braced for a torrent of emotions from my client; we had been working together for several years, and I knew how much the memory of her parents meant to her. I was certain she would want to save the dress, despite its condition: It was yellowed and stained from improper storage, and I was sure her guilt over not caring for it would force her to keep it.

But after a few minutes of consideration, my client impressed me like never before: She said, "Y'know, I have photos of Mom in this dress, and it would be better to remember it as beautiful as it was then. Let's toss it." I checked several times to be sure she was sure, and then it went into a bag and was gone.

Bottom Line: Teach them to decide, and don't dictate what the decision should be.

5/50   Avoiding Technology

Hate technology? Too bad! It's a necessary evil, so learn to use it.

Sorry to be so blunt, but it's true: Email, the internet, smartphones, computers in general—all forms of technology—are the way of the business world and have been for some time now, so it's no longer an option to avoid them. Clients and business associates expect you to have a computer and be proficient in using it; to have an email address, a website, and at least one professional social media account; to know how to search the internet for information; and to know at least the basics of web meeting programs like Zoom, Skype, and GoToMeeting.

If you're gnashing your teeth and bracing to be pulled kicking and screaming into the Information Age, consider the advantages that technology will give you (even if you still hate it):

24/7 access

Thanks to email and messaging apps, clients can communicate with you, and you with them, in an ongoing conversation that does not require you to be present together at the same time. Before the introduction of electronic correspondence, letters through the mail were the most common example of this "asynchronous" communication; email revolutionized the model by shortening the delivery window from days to an instant, and texting took it a step farther. More broadly, this asynchronous connectivity also allows you to do research and shop at your convenience, without leaving your desk and without worrying about store or library hours, the unpleasant surprise of an empty store shelf, or a clerk's mood or knowledge. It also gives you the ability to take time with what you say and therefore communicate exactly what you mean (something we don't always accomplish in real-time conversations).

Cheaper, faster marketing

Email eliminates postage fees. A website eliminates storefront rent. Targeted web-based advertising is more affordable than traditional advertising and provides feedback in the form of analytic data that shows you the impact of each ad you run.

More and faster payment options

When I started my business, accepting credit card payments required purchasing or leasing a bulky portable terminal with its own cellular data account and paying hundreds of dollars a month in fees in addition to per-transaction fees. Now clients can send me an electronic payment instantaneously through Zelle, PayPal, Square, Stripe, and many other apps and merchant service providers, all of which have no monthly fee and a very low (or sometimes no) transaction fee, and I don't have to be present with the client to swipe their card through a machine. What a massive process improvement.

Bottom Line: You might never learn to love it, but you must learn to use technology.

6/50   Being Too Generous

If you have an altruistic nature, you're not alone in this field. PO/PCs tend to be nurturers—"givers"—and we usually get back great rewards in job satisfaction and client appreciation. The downside of generosity, though, is that we sometimes make it easy for people to take advantage of us, even when they don't intend to.

This is one of those instances where your approach to client work and the needs of your business can come into conflict. Some businesspeople laugh at the things I do for clients at no charge: I take their calls between sessions, I look up products on the internet, I bring them relevant articles, I don't charge for the 5 or 10 minutes that some keep me there, chatting, after every session. I've even been known to call a client from a store if I've spotted something I think they might like and offer to pick it up for them.

To me, it's just being nice. To others, it's bad business.

So, in spirit, I'm not the right person to advise you against being too generous with clients, because I'm guilty of it myself. Nonetheless, I feel duty-bound to warn you that all the extra kindnesses can sometimes become a problem.

Some questions to consider regarding the little things you do:

- I'm not making money when I perform unpaid services, but is it also costing me money? Could I instead be working for pay with a client? Could I be putting time into writing an article, making a video, or developing a course?

- Are unpaid services cutting into my administrative time and making it harder to complete my business-maintenance tasks?
- Have clients come to expect that they won't be charged for that 15 minutes that we ran over, or that pack of Post-its that I supplied, or my time to drop off their donations?
- Am I answering clients' texts and social media comments at all hours and allowing myself to be available during personal time?
- Am I giving the impression that my services are less valuable than they are?

While you're at it, think beyond generosity to clients:

- Have my peers' requests for time and free advice from me become burdensome?
- Is my volunteer work crowding out the time I have available for billable hours? Am I on too many committees?

Bottom Line: Think about the extras you do and, if you need to, set boundaries that are a bit firmer so you can continue to be generous without giving until it hurts.

7/50 Ignoring the Need for Business Knowledge

The most common mistake among small business owners in any field is believing that, because you know your product or service very well, you can automatically make a business of it.

As a PO/PC, it's true that you need to have excellent organizing skills in order to succeed, but equally important is the knowledge of how to run a business. Some people in the PO/PC field are employed by a firm or a retailer, but the majority of us are sole proprietors: We're the talent *and* we're the boss.

Instinct and enthusiasm for your craft can take you far in finding creative solutions to business dilemmas and in developing the critical marketing and networking systems that you'll need to gain and retain clients. That's fortunate because you might find the organizing exciting and the business side of things, well, kind of boring. That's understandable. But you really do need to invest at least a small amount of effort into learning the basics about running your company.

If you've ever painted a room, you know that the prep work is drudgery and the painting is quick and fun, but if you skimp on the prep, your result will be sub-par. The same goes for tending to the business side of your business: Do a good job with your prep work so you can make the most of your time with clients.

Spend an afternoon searching the internet for "small business advice," "small business marketing," "micro-companies" (very small businesses, often like ours), and other topics relevant to your operations. Check out the Small Business Administration's website for lots of free advice.

Schedule time each week to tend to business-development tasks such as finding insurance, writing a client agreement, creating a website for your company, contacting local media, and learning about the financial recordkeeping needs of a small business. This isn't the exhilarating, challenging, stimulating side of your duties—this is the sometimes tedious but absolutely crucial foundation-building that will sustain your business into the future.

Bottom Line: You need to spend some time working *on* your business, not just *in* your business.

8/50   Apologizing for Your Fees

I still remember my first client appointment: What a bizarre sensation it was to go to a stranger's house, offer my opinion for a few hours, and walk out with a check written to me from the client. No payroll company, no two-week waiting period, no tax withholding—this was direct and immediate compensation for my expertise and validation of the value of my work.

I immediately felt guilty for taking her money.

After all, I just talked to her about stuff that comes naturally to me, and I helped her move some things and get rid of some things. She needed my help and I gave it. Isn't that just the nice thing to do? Am I selfish for requiring money to do this? What if next week she tells me she has no money—will I refuse to work? Who could be so heartless?!? Argh!!

If you felt the same way with your first client (or if you haven't yet had a client), quick, remember that this is a business! Yes, you're doing important, sometimes life-changing work and you're providing assistance that often cannot be found anywhere else. Hear this: Charging a fee to provide that assistance does not diminish the goodness of it!

Look at it this way: If you didn't get paid to do this work, how could you afford to do it? Unless you're funded by a charitable foundation, your business needs income from its clients in order to sustain itself and to sustain you, its personnel.

It's crucial that you internalize the belief that charging a fee is not bad. If you feel guilty about it, that attitude will come through in your demeanor when you collect payments, discuss rates with prospective clients, or, heaven forbid, when a client fails to pay you and you must call or write to persuade them to send a payment.

If you want to offer a sliding scale or some pro bono services, create a structure for how clients will qualify for those discounts and set a limit in your own budget for how much you can afford to give. If you prefer not to do that, or for times when your discounted hours are full, familiarize yourself with some good websites, online courses, and books on organizing that you could refer people to if they're not able to afford your fee. Knowing that you have these options available and that you have a built-in limit frees you from guilt over turning people away and makes it easier to adhere to your business plan.

Finally, consider posting your rates on your website, so prospective clients can see right away whether you fit into their budgets. This saves them the embarrassment of asking only to find they can't afford to hire you, and it spares you the pain of having to say no to someone in need.

Bottom Line: You deserve to be paid for your services.

9/50   Missing Clients' Nonverbal Cues

You can learn a lot by watching your clients. Without saying a word, clients can tell you when they're confused, frustrated, bored, offended, angry, tired, discouraged, or afraid. You can make your work together more effective if you recognize and acknowledge these nonverbal cues.

The next time you sense that a client has something on their mind, try saying this:

"It looks like you might be feeling [insert descriptor] . . ."

Consider this sentence carefully. Saying "it looks like you might be . . ." is not the same as saying "I can see that you are . . . ," which implies that you've already reached a conclusion, and it's not the same as asking, "Are you feeling . . . ?," which requires the client to answer you.

By saying "it looks like you might be feeling" tired, or overwhelmed, or uncomfortable, or whatever it is you suspect, you acknowledge that you've observed something, that you know your observation might or might not be correct, and that you're inviting the client to discuss it if they wish, but they're also free not to answer.

This is a variation on a technique called "reflective listening," in which you paraphrase and reflect back to the speaker what you think they're saying. For example, if a client becomes very tense when showing you some paperwork, you might say, "It seems like this paperwork is causing you a lot of stress." This statement shows the client that you're listening and trying to understand, that your mindset is empathy and not judgment, and that you are open to hearing more if they want to explain further. Once the client responds, you can move right into solutions by saying something like, "Paperwork is a big stressor for a lot of my clients, and they usually find that creating a filing system really helps. Would you like us to do that?"

Reflective listening is an important skill when working one-on-one with clients, especially chronically disorganized clients. When you validate a client's feelings, it allows the client to acknowledge those feelings as well, which is an important step toward being able to "hear" you and put your suggestions to use.

That said, it's important to understand that reflective listening is not "therapy"; it's used by counselors but it's also a component of coaching and consulting. Therapy focuses on scrutinizing the past by examining emotions. Coaching is future-focused: It acknowledges the impact of feelings while moving toward a specific goal—in this case, getting organized!

Bottom Line: Get good at acknowledging the elephant in the room.

10/50   Falling for the Free-Consultation Trap

I used to offer a free, one-hour, in-person consultation for any prospective client. Nothing terrible happened, but I changed that policy when I realized that I really resented it.

I'm pretty generous with my clients, but this crossed the line with me. A one-hour freebie often meant an additional two hours of driving. It took time out of my schedule that could have been spent on deskwork or with another client. It felt somewhat unsafe to go to people's homes after spending just enough time on the phone to get their name and address.

Worst of all, it sometimes became a contest of wills if the prospective client turned out to be what we sometimes irreverently call a "tire kicker." Tire kickers have you out for a free consultation and want you to tell them everything you would do if they hired you, but they have no intention of hiring you. It might sound like they're interviewing you for the job, but they just want your ideas so they can attempt to implement them themselves.

Side note: You don't have to tell prospective clients exactly what you would do in a particular closet, room, or file drawer. It is legitimate to say, "I have several ideas that might work here, and I'm sure we'll be able to agree on one that will suit your needs."

Nowadays I offer a free consultation by phone or Zoom.

When a prospective client reaches out, I have a conversation with them to find out what their needs are, explain my services and how I work, answer questions, and let them decide during that time whether or not to schedule an appointment. They almost always do, because by that point they're satisfied that I know what I'm talking about, they can trust me, and I'm going to do my best to help them.

I'm completely comfortable with this. I don't have to incur unpaid travel time, I can end a call much easier than I can extract myself from a chatty person's home, I still get a clear idea of whether I'll be able to help the person, and I don't have to deal with tire kickers. The client gets that initial free attention, and we both have the security of "meeting" for the first time by audio or video call. When the client makes an appointment, I can arrive ready to roll up my sleeves and get to work, and I don't feel resentful because I'm being compensated appropriately for my time.

Bottom Line: If you resent giving free consultations (or any other aspects of your business), reduce or eliminate them. Resentment is not a good way to begin a client relationship.

11/50   Disregarding the Importance of Discretion

What do you do to safeguard your clients' privacy? Do you emphasize confidentiality in your dealings with clients and take steps to ensure it? You'd better: If sensitive information about a client leaks out and that leak can be traced back to you, not only will you have lost the client's trust and respect, but oh boy, can you ever be sued!

You have both an ethical and a legal obligation to keep your clients' identities and personal information confidential. This means not sharing clients' names with your family, friends, peers, or anyone else not directly involved in work with that client. If your client is well known, resist the urge to name-drop: It's unbecoming of you, detrimental to your reputation, and unfair to the client.

Maintaining confidentiality also requires protecting your files and records against snoops and refraining from behaviors that would identify a person as your client against their will. Some things that can cause problems with confidentiality:

- Clients' names written in your planner
- Company signs or lettering on your vehicle or clothing
- Client names, payment information, or session notes visible to your accountant, computer tech, or another user of your computer
- Discussing a client case with peers using so much detail that the person could be recognized

- Introducing yourself to a client's visitor or coworker as their PO/PC
- Greeting a client in public

Give some thought to how your procedures impact your clients' privacy and look for ways to improve your confidentiality measures.

At the same time, consider what would qualify as an exception to these policies. What about your personal safety when working in clients' spaces? Are there ways to give a trusted person the ability to see your last known location if you go missing without giving them access to all of your client data? Get creative in figuring this out before the need arises. For more information on confidentiality and personal safety, check out my books on ethics and safety for organizers listed on page 102.

Bottom Line: We have an ethical mandate to uphold client confidentiality.

12/50   Making Clients Beg

In the movie *The Tao of Steve,* the main character shares this bit of wisdom: "We pursue that which retreats from us." He was referring to a phenomenon of dating, but some people use this as a sales strategy.

If you make yourself seem very busy and difficult to reach, the theory goes, people will think you must be the best and they will try even harder to hire you. Convince them that they simply must have you—and that they might not be able to—and you'll have them eating out of your hand. Then, once you do allow them the privilege of hiring you, make it clear that if they don't do things your way, you'll leave and never come back.

I'm no good at this. I don't believe in it, first of all, but I don't think I could pull it off even if I wanted to. I try to return voicemails and emails as quickly as possible (sometimes it does take a few days, but I'm not delaying on purpose). If I think I can help prospective clients, I give them the next available appointment; if it's going to be a while, I explain why that is and I give them suggestions for what they can do in the meantime until we're able to meet. Once we've begun working together, if they don't do their "homework," I don't scold them or issue ultimatums.

When I posted the first, fledgling version of my website, I included a section listing my rates, and I heard that some PO/PCs were displeased with me for doing that. However, I got overwhelmingly positive feedback from prospective clients. They told me they appreciated not having to call and risk embarrassment by asking the price, only to discover that it was far too expensive for them. They said they resented companies that forced them to enter into a conversation first, which struck them as manipulative. By the time they called or emailed me, they already knew whether my services would fit their budget, and in most cases they were ready to make an appointment.

Perhaps, for me, this means that I lose business with prospective clients who really do pursue the PO/PC who retreats from them. This technique must work for some people or they wouldn't advocate it. Maybe they get the clients who think this way, and I get the ones who prefer a more direct approach. In any case, my way works for me, and you need to figure out what suits you best.

Bottom Line: It's up to you to decide how upfront you'll be about your availability and rates, and whether or not you want to make clients pursue you. Just make sure that whatever approach you choose has more benefits than drawbacks.

13/50   Feeding In to Misperceptions

The industry of professional organizing has existed since the 1980s (and productivity consulting for many decades more), but they have only recently exploded in popularity and public awareness. To many people, hiring someone to help them get organized still seems like a new idea. And with the dawning of a new idea comes a host of related misperceptions. Here are some you're likely to face:

When a client thinks getting organized will happen overnight

Shows like *Mission: Organization* and *Clean Sweep* brought unprecedented attention to the field of professional organizing, and we're all grateful for that. Unfortunately, they also gave many people (both clients and new PO/PCs) the impression that getting organized is a quick process. It's not. It is not uncommon to work with a single client every week for a number of years just to reduce and sort their accumulated belongings. You can think of it like this: Real-life organizing is like diet and exercise; TV organizing is like liposuction.

When clients think your job is to swoop in and force them to get rid of stuff

This is another unfortunate side effect of the organizing TV shows and to an even more harmful extreme with the wave of hoarding shows. You'll have to reassure some leery prospective clients that they will retain full control over the decision to keep or toss. And make sure you understand this yourself as well!

When you think it's your fault that a client isn't making progress

If nothing you suggest seems to work, it's most likely because the client is not ready to change, not because none of your ideas are valid. It's okay to tell a client that you think they need more time to get emotionally ready for the organizing process, and to suggest that you should stop for now and touch base in a few months. If you think it might be simply that your personalities are mismatched, you could also offer a referral to another PO/PC.

When people misinterpret what you actually do

People often think that "professional organizer" is another name for housekeeper. In heavily unionized parts of the country, you might even be confused with a labor organizer. (Yes, that happened to me.) Some folks will simply have no clue what a professional organizer or productivity consultant could possibly be. One of your greatest challenges in this business will be educating the people who need your help but don't know such help is available.

Bottom Line: It's your job to anticipate and correct misperceptions about your services.

14/50   Underestimating Your Impact

I realized just how much influence I have the day I saw a note propped up on a client's desk that read, "WWDD?" Instead of WWJD for "What would Jesus do?," a popular mantra at the time, she found it most pertinent, in the midst of organizing her office, to ask herself, "What would Debbie do?"

I was thunderstruck. Of course, she didn't mean that I was more important than God, but the fact that someone would create a constant reminder to try to think like I think. . . . Wow, that's influence.

Know that you have the same power with your clients. Whether you think so or not, whether they indicate it or not, they are watching every single move you make: every facial expression, every word you say, every change in your body language or tone of voice.

Your responses, both spoken and unspoken, register deeply with your clients. Your advice, your speculation or random thoughts, your attitude and reaction to their clutter— everything you say and do speaks volumes to your clients and goes directly to both your effectiveness and their self- esteem.

There's no need to let this intimidate you. Just be aware of it and try to be conscious of the messages you're sending during your time with clients.

I'm careful to say precisely what I mean, but I also try to remain cognizant of my nonverbal messages. If I have a headache and it's making me squint, I tell my client so they won't think I'm angry or impatient. If I'm cold, I try not to cross my arms, because that posture can be construed as defensive or judgmental.

If we're working on filing and the client sees me studying a bank statement, I mention that I'm looking for the date so they won't think I'm snooping. If we encounter something unpleasant or embarrassing for the client, such as a dead mouse in the basement or their dirty underwear on the floor, I'm careful to keep my facial expression neutral because I know that a disgusted or judgmental look from me could be devastating to them.

It's not arrogant to realize that you have a profound impact on your clients. On the contrary, it's humble. It helps you to recognize the great responsibility you carry.

Bottom Line: Know your power and exercise it responsibly.

15/50 Overspending on Advertising

This was an expensive mistake for me. When I started my business in 1997, I thought, "A Yellow Pages ad. . . . Obviously, anyone in business needs a Yellow Pages ad! I'd better get one!" I signed on for several ads in the books covering my geographic area.

Long story short, it didn't pay off, for several reasons: First, at the time, most people didn't know what a professional organizer was, so they didn't use the Yellow Pages to find one. Second, the cost of the ads would have been quite high even if they were bringing me business. Third, I found that other marketing methods—my website, networking with the right groups, referrals from clients—were more effective and more cost-effective. Fourth, to have Yellow Pages ads I also had to have a business landline phone (not just a residential or cellphone number), which was an added expense I wouldn't have needed otherwise.

Worst of all, when I moved to a new home and changed my phone service, I was unaware that my Yellow Pages contract would become payable in full immediately. It had appeared as a monthly charge of several hundred dollars on my phone bill. When I changed my service, they made me pay several thousand dollars all at once—no deals, no negotiation. Do I wish I had seen this coming? Absolutely!

The lessons learned from this now-extinct paper advertising medium still apply to today's online advertising options: Think very carefully before you commit yourself to advertising that is expensive and/or that involves a long-term contract. In fact, look into what you can accomplish on your own and with very little risk, through options like Google Ads and social media advertising, before you pay a third party to set up online advertising for you. For that matter, remember that your website, social media accounts, and networking are all forms of marketing with likely better returns than paid ads.

If you're unsure or intimidated, check with peers: Has the option you're considering paid off for them? If you do opt to work with an advertising vendor, get specific, granular statistics from them regarding the value of this ad for people in your geographic area and in the PO/PC industry. If they can't show you that the ad will pay for itself in business, don't buy it! I've had more than one such salesperson try to convince me that I should invest in a billboard. Seriously. A billboard. Keep your wits about you in these meetings.

As you venture into paid advertising, start slowly. Try one type at a time, and begin with less expensive, no-contract options like budget-capped social media campaigns to get a feel for what's going to work for you. Be sure to review all of the analytics available to you about the ad's performance so you can continually hone your approach and improve the effectiveness of your future ads.

Bottom Line: Exhaust all modern, low-cost, no-contract options before you resort to expensive traditional forms of advertising.

16/50   Depriving Your Clients of Empathy

This is one of my "soapbox issues." Some colleagues tell me that they can hear me mentally dragging out my soapbox and gearing up for a lecture when someone speaks insensitively about a client. You might think I'm nice for writing this book and giving you all of this advice. True, I'm happy to see other PO/PCs succeed, because success for any one of us benefits us all on a global level. But it's not just for you that I do this, dear colleague. I'm doing it for your clients.

My top priority in this business is our clients. I am highly protective of them. Since I work mostly with chronically disorganized clients, mine tend to be the ones who are most in need of empathy—hence my emphasis on this issue. But I will also defend your clients, or anyone's clients, if I hear someone talking about them insensitively. I hope most fervently that you will do the same.

Whether your clients are chronically disorganized or not, every one of them comes to you in need. They need your organizing expertise, and along with that, they need you to empathize with their situation. They do not need, nor do they want, nor do they deserve judgment, condescension, marginalization, or disrespect.

Your clients will not thrive without empathy. If you can't give it, you will not be able to do your best work and, worse still, you risk doing harm.

Our clients might not have the innate organizing abilities that we possess, but they have skills in other areas and they excel at things that we do not. Some of them might seem like they could do this if they would just get motivated, and therein lies a critical point: It's not our place to gauge how hard they're trying (and therefore how deserving they are of our assistance or approval). What can be observed in a client, or in anyone for that matter, is rarely the entire story; we have no way of knowing what goes on in their heads and what physical, mental, or emotional processes might be helping or hindering their motivation.

Sometimes new PO/PCs don't realize how they sound when they talk about their work. Saying things like "I can't believe people live like this!" might be a true reflection of your feelings, but can you see why it would sound insensitive? Instead, how about, "I'm shocked by the severity of some clients' situations, and I'm worried that I won't be able to help them." That underlying worry is the real issue anyway, right?

Bottom Line: If you're unable to offer empathy to someone, do not take that person on as a client.

17/50   Focusing on Dollar Signs

This one can cause trouble in so many ways. It should come as no surprise that in the organizing and productivity industry, just like in every other area of life, if you get too caught up in moneymoneymoney you might find yourself doing unethical things to get it.

Selling organizing products

It's fine to sell your own product or to resell products made by others. It's not fine to encourage all of your clients to buy your product, regardless of whether it's right for them. (Fact: There is no single product that is right for everyone.)

Searching for "cash cow" clients

It's fine to work with clients over a long period of time. Regular clients do provide stability in our business, and many people need long-term coaching. It's not okay to think of them as "cash cows" and to continue to milk them long after their need for you has passed. We should be teaching our clients to be as self-sufficient as possible, not trying to make them dependent on us for life.

Making money from their discards

It's fine to encourage clients to discard unneeded clutter. It's also fine to dispose of it for them by taking it to be donated or putting it in a resale shop on their behalf. It's not okay to take that stuff and, unbeknownst to the client, resell it yourself and keep the money.

Targeting wealthy clients so you can charge more

It's fine to focus your marketing efforts in geographic areas or economic sectors where you know there are people who can afford your fees. It's not okay to target rich people with the intention of jacking up your prices when you see how big their houses are.

Bottom Line: Don't let greed interfere with ethical business practices.

18/50   Missing Out on Free Advice

Thank goodness for Don!

Don was my first Small Business Development Center advisor. The SBDC is a free program sponsored by the U.S. government's Small Business Administration. Don gave me free advice for over 15 years, from before I founded my company until I moved out of state.

When I knew nothing other than that I wanted to start an organizing business, Don walked me through the basics: register your name, figure out what to charge, decide how and where to market your services. At various points along the way, when I had big decisions to make or found new opportunities to expand my business, Don steered me in the right direction.

Don helped me the way I hope I'm helping you: He warned me about pitfalls and got me back on track when I hit one.

Great news for Americans: You can have your very own Don! Go to the SBDC website (www.sba.gov/sbdc as of this writing) and search for the Small Business Development Center in your area. There are over 900 SBDCs across the country. The website itself also has lots of useful information, so check out some of the resources available to you online as well.

It's not often that we can truly get something for nothing. Why do they do it? To support the government's efforts to stimulate economic growth in the small-business sector. It might often seem like the cards are stacked against small businesses, but sometimes the little guy or gal really can catch a break. Don't miss out on this great opportunity for no-charge guidance and mentoring from knowledgeable and impartial counselors.

Bonus: The SBA and SBDCs can direct you to many other helpful programs in addition to their own.

Bottom Line: As a small business owner, there is a wealth of information and assistance available to you. All you have to do is ask for it!

19/50   Biting Off More Than You Can Chew

Sometimes your enthusiasm writes checks that your abilities can't cash. Maybe it's a project that you feel ill-equipped to complete, or maybe you scheduled too many clients all at once. Either way, you're really sweating now. What to do?

If you don't take on new challenges, how can you learn new skills? It's true that you should challenge yourself and not be afraid to take your abilities to new heights. Just be careful not to bluff with clients and give them the impression that you're more experienced than you are. It's fine to be honest and say, "I've never faced this challenge before, but let's try to solve it together!"

These are times when your budding peer relationships will come in very handy. Ask colleagues if they've handled a similar project; depending on how close of friends you've become, it might be best to offer your colleague a consultation fee in exchange for advice. They might not accept it, but they'll appreciate the offer.

Also consider reaching beyond your close circle. If you're a member of the National Association of Productivity & Organizing Professionals, you could post a question to the NAPO online discussion forum. Also look into other groups for PO/PCs such as Organizer.Club, specialty groups including the Institute for Challenging Disorganization and National Association of Senior Move Managers, or member groups outside the U.S. including Associação Nacional de Profissionais de Organização e Produtividade (Brazil),

Professional Organizers in Canada, Associazione Professional Organizers Italia (Italy), Japanese Association of Life Organizers, Korea Association of Professional Organizers, Nederlands Beroepsvereniging van Professional Organizers (Netherlands), and Association of Professional Declutterers and Organisers (United Kingdom).

What if the problem isn't the type of work but the amount of it? In the beginning, I scheduled two clients a day, Monday through Friday—one 1-4pm and the other 6-9pm. Friends teased me about only working 6 hours a day, and for a while I bought into their flawed perception. The reality was that I was *billing* for just 6 hours a day but, with travel time and administrative tasks, I was working at least 10 hours *every* day, not just weekdays. At least I was wise enough not to schedule clients on the weekends on top of all that.

I was totally fried. Something had to give, so I began scheduling just one client a day. Once in a while, if two clients really needed to see me, I would double-book a day, but I tried to make that the exception to the rule. I used the other block of time each day to develop other revenue streams, such as my courses and the book you're reading now, and to keep up with admin work, my volunteer responsibilities . . . and laundry.

Bottom Line: Don't be afraid to slow down, catch your breath, and ask for help.

20/50   Not Understanding Special-Needs Clients

Some folks just want you to organize their closets; others need much more specialized intervention.

Some people are "chronically disorganized" (CD), perhaps because they have attention deficit/hyperactivity disorder (AD/HD), depression, or anxiety. Physical disabilities, especially those that cause chronic pain and/or sleep disturbances (such as fibromyalgia and chronic fatigue syndrome) and conditions that are common among elderly clients (such as arthritis) are often present with CD and will make organizing more challenging. People who are grieving also need specialized care, as do those with the most advanced challenge: hoarding.

One thing that special-needs clients tend to have in common is a more emotional response to your work together. Organizing can bring up feelings of shame, inadequacy, anger, regret, and more, and you need to be ready to deal with these feelings with compassion. If this makes you uncomfortable, that's okay: All that's required of you is to do no harm in your response and to connect the client with a specialized PO/PC.

Serving special-needs clients is definitely not for everyone. If it's not your passion, you should not do it, for the client's wellbeing and your own. Learn which of your colleagues work with particular special needs and be ready to refer clients to them.

If you want to work with special-needs clients, learn as much as you can about the most effective ways to relate to them and help them with their organizing projects. The most comprehensive source for this knowledge is the Institute for Challenging Disorganization. ICD offers courses on dozens of topics including how to work with clients who hoard in a manner that is safe for both the client and yourself. ICD is also a membership organization with a deeply knowledgeable and experienced community where you can explore and discuss the variety of conditions that can cause or coexist with chronic disorganization and effective ways to help CD clients.

To continue your education specific to AD/HD, peruse the information and resources available through the Attention Deficit Disorder Association (ADDA) and Children and Adults with Attention-Deficit/Hyperactivity Disorder (CHADD).

NAPO has also begun to expand their curriculum with courses on special needs, including a Brain-Based Conditions track for which I contributed the course "Ethics and Policies for Working with Clients with Brain-based Conditions."

Bottom Line: Even if you choose not to work with special-needs or CD clients, it's important to know enough about them to make a referral to another PO/PC and not inadvertently worsen the situation or harm the client with your inexperience.

21/50   Saying Yes to Everything

Ever heard that expression "Jack of All Trades"? Sounds like a compliment until you hear the full title: "Jack of All Trades and Master of None." As you begin your professional organizing career, it's great to try out every specialty that interests you. Eventually, though, you'll probably find it most efficient and fulfilling to focus on one or two areas of specialization that you love and do really well.

I've always focused on chronically disorganized clients, but over the years I've had to scale back the services that I offer them. One example is closet remodeling. I used to install modular closet systems for my clients, from dismantling the existing system to shopping for the new components to installing them, even custom-cutting shelves to create a closet that was a perfect fit for the space.

Another example is heavy lifting. I've carried desks on my back, all by myself, for clients who lacked the strength to help. I've gotten bookcases up and down stairwells, moved furniture to plug in computers, climbed on roofs and crawled through attics, and hauled out umpteen overstuffed trash bags and boxes. Why, you might be asking, horrified? Partly because I'm strong, and partly because I'm both impatient and stubborn. When I see a need, gosh darn it, I fill it.

Alas, my sacroiliac does not dig this heroism. I've had to stop with the closets and the furniture in deference to my lower back, which has a most unpleasant way of forcing me to cease and desist. I've discovered a lifting limit for myself, and it's around 30 pounds. But, the upside is that I've gotten even better at the things I still do.

You might think I'm going to tell you not to lift so your own back won't get hinky. Nope, you go right ahead if you want to. My advice on this point is more global: If you find one day that you're no longer able to do something you once could, accept it and find another way. Don't keep trying and end up doing permanent damage. This goes for limitations in your physical abilities, and—here's a twist—it also applies to your client relationships. In all aspects of your work, be ready to call it quits when it's time; then you'll be free to focus more on what you do best.

Bottom Line: A niche is a good thing. It's supportive, it's got boundaries, it's a manageable size. Find a niche you like and make the most of it.

22/50   Combining Project and Coaching Models

This one is not forbidden per se, but it's ill-advised because it takes an excessive amount of planning, discipline, and schedule contortions to make it work. Allow me an extended metaphor. . . .

Suppose you're a roofer. You generally complete one roof at a time, working all day every day until it's finished, and then you move on to the next roof. You don't do 3 square feet of each of a dozen roofs once a week until they're done; your partially completed work would be compromised by weather and animals in the meantime, and the owner would be seriously inconvenienced.

Now suppose you're a gardener. You have a roster of gardens that you visit on a regular rotation to prune and fertilize and encourage to grow into the owner's vision. You don't simply trim the hedges, apply weed killer, and call it complete; no garden can thrive on a one-and-done intervention.

Now suppose you're both a roofer and gardener. What would your workday look like? How would you do both of those jobs thoroughly and well?

In the organizing and productivity industry, structuring your business according to the Project Model is like being a roofer: You complete a project for one client and then begin one with someone new. The Coaching Model is like being a gardener: working with a number of clients concurrently, in shorter sessions over a number of weeks, months, or even years.

Trying to work with both project clients and coaching clients makes it difficult to accommodate the scheduling needs of each, because those needs will often conflict.

I specialize in coaching chronically disorganized clients. For my business, this means shorter client sessions (usually one to two hours at a time) over a longer span of time (often several years), and many of my clients book regularly recurring appointments (every Monday afternoon, every other Wednesday, etc.).

This means I'm not available for full-time projects such as relocations, which would require me to work with one client for, say, five days in a row, eight hours each day. If I did, my "regulars" wouldn't get to see me at their usual times.

Bottom Line: Choose either the Project Model or the Coaching Model, based on the types of organizing jobs you prefer, and fill your appointment schedule accordingly.

23/50   Vouching for Other People

I learned this one the hard way. As a PO/PC, I'm often asked for referrals to doctors, lawyers, therapists, accountants, electricians, moving companies, and on and on. I keep a long list of such individuals and companies, and I offer their names and numbers readily whenever a client is in need. The important part is how I offer those contacts.

When I make a referral for a client, I am careful to tell the client exactly what I know—and don't know—about the third party.

If the third party is a friend of mine, I say so. If it's someone I met at a networking event but whose work I haven't experienced firsthand, I make sure the client understands that. If it's someone whose services I have used, I tell my client that I worked with the person and whether they were satisfactory for me, but I never, ever guarantee a third party's performance.

You can even give a referral with a caveat, such as, "This guy is great at what he does, but frankly, he's got a difficult personality. If you think you can handle that, I'll give you his number."

Once upon a time, I hired a contractor who did excellent work for me: a roof and a porch on my old house and a beautiful new office in my new house. When one of my best clients needed a contractor, I recommended this guy with the highest possible praise.

The client called him and got the runaround. A month later I found out the contractor had developed a drinking problem and skipped town to escape paying thousands of dollars owed to his subcontractors.

Luckily my client never got through to that contractor, but whoa—close call!

Bottom Line: If you're going to make referrals to other service providers, take care not to exaggerate their greatness, and never make promises about their performance. Instead, give your client enough information to make their own informed choice.

24/50 Trying to Be All Things to All Clients

Our clients see us as experts, and rightly so. But there's this phenomenon called the "halo effect" that often makes clients think we are experts in everything, not just organizing or productivity.

Sure, it's flattering. We like it when people value our opinions, whether on storage containers or workflows or tax laws or medications . . . hey, wait a minute. . . .

We must be very careful not to cross into areas of expertise that are not our own. Often clients do need advice or assistance with legal issues, medical issues, financial issues, and a host of other specialties. It can be highly tempting to try to fill those needs, particularly when we know the client has a limited budget, and especially if we've managed these same issues in our own lives, for ourselves or our children or parents.

Nonetheless, we have to keep our professional boundaries clear. What we're competent or brave or desperate enough to try in our personal lives is usually broader in scope than what we're competent to do professionally.

If you're not a therapist, don't try to be one to your clients. If you're not an attorney, don't give legal advice. If you're not a plumber, veterinarian, or hazardous waste expert, don't tell clients what to do with leaking pipes, vomiting dogs, or that little bottle of mercury that's been in the garage for time out of mind.

Don't risk being wrong: Give a referral. We provide great added value to our clients by referring them to other experts and keeping our amateur opinions to ourselves.

Bottom Line: We can't solve every one of our clients' problems. Know which issues are within your scope and which require a referral to another expert.

25/50   Failing to Establish Clear Policies

I have a Client Agreement that I give to every new client which outlines my company policies on things like cancellations, safe working conditions, confidentiality, and situations that are and are not acceptable (e.g. it's fine to have friends present while we work; it's not fine to do vodka shots with those friends while we work).

Every one of the policies in that document has a story behind it that represents a point at which I had to firm up a boundary with a client.

When I started my company, my goals were, and still are, to be as helpful and flexible as I possibly can. The difference is in how my definition of "as I possibly can" has evolved.

In the beginning, if I felt resentful of or uncomfortable with something I was doing for a client or with something the client was doing or not doing, that initial emotion led me right into feeling guilty and spoiled. It took some time to accept the fact that, like it or not, there are limits to what I can or am willing to do, and that trying to ignore those boundaries erodes my effectiveness and in turn makes the client uncomfortable.

Over time, I began to respect my boundaries and to document them in my client agreement. Stating them clearly has been cathartic for me, and it gives the client more freedom because they know from the beginning what is okay with me and what's not.

For example, I have a very liberal cancellation policy, but a very strict rule against working in a space infested with vermin. I offer a lot of latitude in cancellations because I'm comfortable doing so, and I refuse to work in spaces with bedbugs or roaches because it would be unsafe for myself and for other clients to whom I could carry them. (And yes, also because it's revolting.)

More examples: I have no problem with clients and family members displaying emotions, but I won't stick around if things get violent. I don't care what novelties might be unearthed in clients' nightstands, but if there's a gun in there they'd better warn me. Friendly pets are great; aggressive ones are unacceptable.

Each of these guidelines helps me to feel sure of what I'm doing and confident that I'm prepared for any situation.

Bottom Line: This work becomes more and more comfortable, for you and for your clients, with each boundary issue you encounter and then resolve with a clearly expressed policy.

26/50   Charging Too Little or Too Much

What to charge is one of the very first questions every new PO/PC ponders, and it's one that will continue to puzzle you from time to time, no matter how long you're in business. There's more to it than simply choosing the highest dollar amount that you think you can get away with. It's better to build a system for determining your prices, then use that system to update your rates as needed.

There are many different ways to develop your pricing strategy. Some key points to consider:

- Whether you will charge by the job or by the hour
- Your realistic average workload (the maximum amount of work you can handle minus an allowance for unbooked time and unforeseen events like cancellations [by the client or by you])
- The amount you need your billable time to earn in order to compensate you for your administrative time (e.g. deskwork, marketing)
- Travel time and other incidentals
- The cost of living in your region

So what happens if you choose the wrong rate? Either way, you won't make enough money.

If your rate is too high, you'll eliminate some clients. Some PO/PCs do this intentionally; if this is you, be careful not to set your price so high that you don't get enough clients to sustain your business, and be VERY careful that your pricing policy is not and cannot be considered discriminatory by ethnicity, age, gender, or perceived wealth of an area.

If your rate is too low, ironically, you're likely to hear more complaints about the cost of your services. When something is inexpensive, people tend to devalue it and therefore find fault with it more often. When a service is expensive enough to require giving up something else, people tend to value that service more because they had to sacrifice to have it. Think of how people will haggle for a fifty-cent discount at a garage sale, but they wouldn't dream of asking their doctor, lawyer, or therapist to "knock a few bucks off."

I'm not telling you to charge high fees; I'm saying that low fees might not make you as popular as you'd think.

Bottom Line: The right rate will pay you what you need to earn, minimize tire-kicking, make you accessible to the clients you want to reach, and be non-discriminatory.

27/50   Selecting the Wrong Company Name

When my mom named me, she chose Deborah. She said she liked that name because it would grow up with me: I could be Debbie as a kid, Deb as an adult, and Deborah when I wanted to be formal. (It was Deborah Ann when I got in trouble!)

The same principle works well for choosing a company name. Look for one that is unique, conveys the professional image you want to project, and can grow with you as your business evolves.

My company's original full name was Red Letter Day Professional Organizers. I chose to make it plural even though I was a one-person operation in the beginning because I figured, sooner or later, I'd have a staff. If you shorten it to Red Letter Day, it still works. It's unusual, memorable, and professional but not intimidating. And it fits well, because a "red letter day" is an important one, one you would write in red on your calendar. My slogan became, "When you get organized, it'll be a Red Letter Day!"

Want to know some of the suggestions I got from others? How about "Debbie Does Organizing"? Oh, great, a pun on the title of an infamous porno film. Yeah, right. Or what about "Debbie's Organizing Service"? Well, it would have done the job, but it definitely sounds like a small operation, maybe even a hobby—not the image I wanted to convey. Oh, hey, why not "Clutter Busters"?!? Cute, catchy, has alliteration . . . and there must already be three dozen separate companies named Clutter Busters. I said no to sexual innuendo, clichés, and small-time imagery.

Before you commit yourself to a company name, make sure it's not already registered by someone in your area. Also do a web search and check the directories of your member associations to make sure you're not duplicating another company's name. Even if you could get away with it legally, the branding confusion and bad blood aren't worth it.

If you already have a company name and you're realizing with dismay that it might not fit you much longer, change it now, before you become even more established. I went back for my counseling degree years after starting my company, so when I became licensed, I changed my company name to Red Letter Day Counseling and Consulting.

If you can't change your company name but you don't like the way it's impacting your image, another option is to add a "d.b.a." ("doing business as"): Over the years, the expression "red letter day" became less common and was causing confusion, so I added the d.b.a. "Thoughts In Order" and now operate under that as my company name, while Red Letter Day remains my legal parent company behind the scenes. D.b.a.s are typically formed through the same government office you used to register your original company name.

Bottom Line: Your choice of company name is highly consequential, so take your time and choose carefully.

28/50   Expecting Free Advice

If you plan to ask a veteran PO/PC for advice, proceed with caution. Most of us don't mind answering a simple question now and then, especially during a NAPO chapter meeting or at the annual conference, but it's not fair to expect step-by-step solutions to your business dilemmas—even if you're the one buying lunch. You'll do well to avoid the expression "pick your brain" . . . when experienced PO/PCs get to venting, that expression is one of the things we complain about. ;)

Keep in mind that many PO/PCs offer peer coaching or consultation for a fee. At first this might sound distasteful to you, but think of it this way: Clients pay us for our time and advice. Shouldn't we offer each other the same courtesy? Whatever you do, never convey an "entitlement attitude." Your peers do not owe you anything; any advice, encouragement, or guidance they give you should be appreciated as a privilege, even if you're paying them for it.

NAPO members who have also joined their local chapter or the worldwide virtual chapter have an extra opportunity to learn from their peers. Chapter meetings are a great place to absorb new information and to get a broader perspective. Some chapters have formal mentoring programs in place; if yours does, take advantage of it! If not, talk to other members and try to establish good peer relationships. Think of something you can offer to offset your taking with some giving.

You might think that an ideal trade would be to offer yourself as a free assistant to an established PO/PC in exchange for mentoring. In some types of client work, this can indeed be a welcomed partnership, but not always. Professionals who work with chronically disorganized or other special-needs clients will most likely be reluctant—or will flat-out refuse—to allow you to "job-shadow."

Why? These types of clients tend to have a much harder time emotionally with the organizing process, so introducing a stranger into the dynamic would be intrusive and could compromise the effectiveness of the client/professional relationship. If you're denied this form of on-the-job training, don't take it personally, and do respect the veteran's concern for the client.

If you're wondering where to draw the line in soliciting free advice, ask yourself how long it will take the other person to answer you. If it's more than 2 minutes, you might be risking an imposition. And never ask for proprietary information, such as a copy of their client agreement. These are items that were constructed through hours of work or fees they paid to other consultants; asking to copy them is asking too much.

Bottom Line: You will likely find that some peers are more willing than others to be helpful to you (just as in any other group). You'll be unlikely to offend if you offer to pay for their advice.

29/50   Neglecting Professionalism

Here's a tricky one: What exactly is "professionalism"? What's professional in one person might not be in someone else. And just to make it more complicated, "professional" does not necessarily mean "formal." How can you tell what's right for you?

As you develop your company's brand (the things for which it is remembered, recognized, and assessed), you will also develop your own individualized approach to speaking and behaving in a professional manner. Some things that can impact your professionalism:

- How you discuss your work with clients, peers, and others
- What you wear to client appointments and business functions
- Whether what you say matches what you do
- How "businesslike" your business seems

The trick to being professional is knowing the impression you're making and adding, subtracting, or changing things until that impression is the one you want to make. Professionalism is highly subjective, so you can't just follow a checklist; you have to figure it out for yourself through trial and error.

There are no rules on exactly what is and is not professional, but there are some guidelines to help you determine whether or not something adds to or detracts from your professionalism:

- Does what you wear send the right message? Everything from jeans to suits has its place in our work.
- How would you feel if clients could hear the way you speak about them? Would you be proud or embarrassed? Would they be impressed or insulted?
- Do you follow through on everything you promise, even implied promises such as being on time or returning calls and emails promptly?
- Do points such as the way you answer the phone and the sounds in the background, the attention to detail in your marketing materials and messaging, and your knowledge of the industry all contribute to your and your company's professional image?
- Is your "brand identity" consistent, or at least not in conflict, across all of your platforms (website, social media accounts, business cards, media appearances, blog posts, etc.)? Whether it's formal or casual, serious or playful, conservative or avant garde, anything can be your version of professional but it needs to be consistent or it will come across as inauthentic.
- If your personal social media accounts include public posts, do they represent you in ways you're okay with being seen by clients, colleagues, and networking contacts?

Bottom Line: Work on establishing what is professional for you and then endeavor to convey a consistently professional image.

30/50   Getting Drunk on Self-Employment

No doubt about it, being your own boss is a power trip. You call the shots, you set the schedule, and you don't have to worry about taking any guff from anyone anymore. Right?

Well, perhaps. But don't start giving guff yourself. It can be easy to bark at people who aren't doing what we want when there's no boss to scowl at us for not being a "team player." Sure, you're the master of your domain now, but you'll get much farther as a kind and benevolent ruler than as a tyrant.

No matter how successful you are, you will still need cooperation from others, whether it's the customer service rep for the phone company or the person behind the window at the county clerk's office or the technician hooking up the A/V for your speech. As my Grandma used to say, "You catch more flies with honey than with vinegar." So be nice!

People do notice how you treat them, but you know what else? Some people even notice how you treat others, and they form their opinion of you accordingly. Many fail to realize that second point: That's why you see so many folks sucking up to the boss at dinner and giving the waiter a hard time.

Here's a book full of wisdom on how to show sincere kindness and appreciation toward your fellow humans: *How to Win Friends and Influence People* by Dale Carnegie. It's really old (although still in print and available) and the language is somewhat outdated now, but the advice has held up just fine.

I keep a list of the "Carnegie Principles" as a note in my phone. Sometimes when I'm about to deal with a difficult person or situation, I skim that list for a reality check on the approach I plan to take.

If my instinct is to lash out at someone who's being an idiot, the Carnegie Principles list snaps me back into giving a more effective response. Sometimes it even makes me think, okay, maybe they're not really an idiot. ;)

Bottom Line: You might not have a boss now, but there will always be people whose opinion of you counts, and you won't always know who they are. Develop a reputation for courtesy and cooperation by treating everyone with respect—not just the bigwigs.

31/50   Joining Every Group

When your business is new, getting your name out there is your top priority, so it's natural to be tempted to join every networking group, community group, and professional association that will have you. Remember that episode of *The Brady Bunch* where Jan, determined to become popular, joins every club in school?

Don't be like Jan. You'll quickly burn yourself out—something a self-employed person cannot afford to do. Before joining a group, consider these questions:

- How much does it cost to join? Are there additional fees besides membership?
- Is the meeting schedule realistic for me?
- Are the other members people who are likely to use my services? Am I likely to use theirs? Or do we all serve similar clients in different ways?
- Will I learn new business skills, have opportunities to teach or give speeches, or gain valuable knowledge from this membership?
- Do the benefits of this membership overlap with one I already have?
- Do I have to do any work (e.g. serve on a committee, volunteer additional time, deliver a quota of referrals) in order to be a member?
- Will membership in this group give me discounts I couldn't otherwise get?
- What would it take to get out of this group if I wanted to?

As of this writing, I am a member of the National Association of Productivity & Organizing Professionals (NAPO) and of both the Michigan and Austin, Texas chapters. I'm also a member of the American Counseling Association, the Recording Academy including the Texas chapter, a local music patronage society called Black Fret, and two local business networking groups.

All of these memberships provide multiple values for me: Networking with peers and professionals doing similar work or doing very different work but with the same clients, referral sharing, leadership roles, continuing education, speaking and teaching opportunities, and discounts on products and services like professional liability insurance.

There are at least three times this many groups that I have joined in the past, have been tempted to join, or would love to have the time to join. Alas, if I joined everything, I'd be broke and I'd have no time for clients!

Bottom Line: Choose your memberships carefully, based on their potential benefits to you.

32/50 Harboring Negative Opinions of Clients

This might just be the touchiest issue I've ever addressed as a PO/PC training other PO/PCs: What do you think of your clients, honestly?

Assuming that you're starting with an appropriate foundation of empathy for the client (and if you're not, that's a different problem), do you put on a friendly face but cringe inside when you see floors and hallways stacked with papers? Do you tell them that a messy desk doesn't necessarily indicate an underachiever (but not quite believe your own words)? Do you say there's no need to "clean up" before your appointment, then mentally take points off when they don't? If a client's home or office is not as clean as you keep yours, do you find yourself not wanting to touch things and avoid using the bathroom?

I'm not here to tell you that you're wrong if you think these things. We've all got decades of preconceptions that affect our first impressions and lasting opinions of everyone we meet. We all have our individual comfort levels regarding cleanliness and clutter, whether with clients' spaces, friends' homes, or public places. As PO/PCs, particularly those of us working with chronically disorganized clients, we might empathize with the reasons for the situation but find it unpleasant nonetheless.

What I want you to understand is that it's very difficult to mask our true feelings. You might think you're pretty good at it, but our clients are even better at reading our faces and language, and they know. I've been doing this work for decades now and I consider myself excellent at maintaining an objective demeanor, which is why I was dismayed when a client pointed out, as we worked on purging her closet, that she could tell when I agreed with her decisions. Perhaps she was just imagining a hint of a smile from me each time she said "toss it"; perhaps she was actually hoping to see my approval. Either way, it unnerved me.

It's unrealistic to expect that you'll never show your true feelings with clients. I think, though, that the right thing to do, for yourself and for them, is to stay within your comfort zone as much as possible. If you can tolerate working in severely disorganized and/or very unclean environments, please do: The people living and working in those spaces desperately need your help. If you can't tolerate it, though, don't force yourself: It's unfair to you and also to clients because your discomfort will reduce your effectiveness and add to their shame.

Bottom Line: Try not to work with clients of whom you have a negative opinion. It's bad for both of you.

33/50   Being Overly Competitive

When the Michigan chapter of NAPO was in its formative months, we were all a little leery of one another. Until then, we'd been lone wolves, practicing our trade in almost complete isolation from one another. Concerns were raised as to how much information we would be sharing with people who were, when it came right down to it, our competition.

I admit I felt it too. I had worked hard to develop my marketing materials, my approach with clients, and every other little detail of my company. I wasn't about to walk into some meeting and hand it all over to novices. Luckily, that request was never made. From the beginning, we settled into a comfortable camaraderie in which everyone shared what they wanted to and kept to themselves what they considered proprietary, and together we quickly discovered that each of us had both things to teach and things to learn from our newly formed community.

In NAPO-MI, we came to realize the truth of NAPO National's contention that "together we are better." When one of us gets press coverage, it increases awareness of the industry for us all. When one PO/PC gets more clients than they can handle, they'll refer some to another PO/PC in the area.

It turns out there really is no need to be ruthlessly competitive in this business; there is enough work to go around. Besides, the business your peers could take from you when you see them as "the enemy" is nothing compared to the benefits you'll lose in failing to develop a cordial working relationship with them.

If you don't make friends among your fellow PO/PCs, who will answer your questions? Who will mentor you or help you figure out tricky client situations? Who will give you new ideas to keep your business growing? For Pete's sake, who will sit with you at the annual conference? ;) It's so much more productive and fun to be part of a group of your peers than it is to be a lone wolf.

Here's an idea: If you don't have a local chapter of NAPO in your area (or even if you do), get involved with NAPO on the national level by volunteering for a committee or task force that interests you. You'll make new connections and expand your list of fellow PO/PCs you can turn to when you need help or advice.

Bottom Line: Cultivating your place in a community will serve you better than going it alone.

34/50   Neglecting Personal Safety

If you work with residential clients, perhaps you've had occasion to feel nervous about going into a stranger's home. Maybe you've felt ill at ease in an office setting too. Even if you haven't had your first client yet, maybe this thought has crossed your mind already.

I teach a course on personal safety for onsite professionals, and each time I present it, I hear a range of experiences: Some people tell me they are constantly fearful of going to clients' homes alone, others say it has never occurred to them to worry, and most are somewhere in the middle. Unfortunately, I've also heard more than a handful of accounts from PO/PCs who have been verbally and physically threatened or assaulted by clients.

It is valid to be concerned for your personal safety with clients and their environments. In fact, I consider it crucial for each of us to carry a healthy amount of apprehension each time we enter a client's space. Every PO/PC, whether a newbie or a veteran, should give thought to the dangers we might encounter, including not only assault by the client or someone else present, but also hazards such as toxic chemicals, disease-carrying vermin, or the possibility of tripping or having things fall on us while working. In 2020, the COVID-19 pandemic added a new level of risk to spending extended time indoors with clients.

Formulate a safety plan. Always carry your cellphone on your person and consider equipping it with one of various apps that can track your whereabouts if you go missing. Think through some possible scenarios and how you would handle them.

Most important, hone your intuition—it is by far your best defense in any dangerous situation. If you have a feeling that something is wrong, even if you can't put your finger on what it is, trust your gut and remove yourself from the situation.

I recommend the book *The Gift of Fear* by Gavin de Becker as an outstanding resource for information on how intuition works and how to learn to trust it. De Becker says "intuition is knowing without knowing why": It's not just hysterical female stuff, as some might say; learning to hear, interpret, and trust your intuition could one day save your life.

When you have that "uh-oh" feeling, stop what you're doing and get out. You can take the time to figure out what you were reacting to later, once you're safe.

For more information on personal safety (and the story of the scary encounter that prompted me to teach safety for PO/PCs), check out my book "*Let Me Show You the Basement*": *A Guide to Staying Safe in Clients' Homes.*

Bottom Line: There are inherent risks in this work, but you can mitigate them with planning and attentiveness.

35/50   Blurring Boundaries with Clients

One of the reasons that clients sometimes think of us as miracle workers is that we succeed in helping them to get organized after friends and family have failed. It makes sense that we would, of course, since we bring ideas and tools that people outside of our profession tend not to have. But that's only part of the story. Another important reason that we are more effective than clients' loved ones is that we are objective outsiders.

Friends and family feel free to us what to do, and not very diplomatically. And we, in turn, feel free to ignore them. That's just how it is when you have history with someone. But when we hire an expert to tell us what to do, we're all ears and pen and notepad. The expert could tell us the same thing as Mom but, coming from a pro, it holds more weight. (And then Mom declares "I told you that for free!" and we, naturally, ignore her.)

I have several organizing clients with whom I would love to be buddies. They're really cool people, and I enjoy their company. Sometimes they invite me to a party or to lunch, and sometimes I go; with some, I exchange emails that include both business questions and updates on personal topics. But overall I keep our relationship professional, because I know that if it transitions into more friendship than client and consultant, it will change how each of us interacts with and reacts to the other, and my effectiveness with them will slip.

If you doubt this, try organizing your mother. (Or if your mother is just as organized as you, or more, go to the next-closest disorganized loved one.) Now just try to treat them like a client.

When I work on weeding out clothing with a client, I'm patient, attentive, objective. I offer organizing theories, make neutral observations regarding the condition of garments, and ask questions designed to help the client decide for themselves.

The one time I tried this with my mother, within a minute I was flinging stuff off hangers onto the floor and exclaiming, "I can't believe you still have these dorky clothes!" So Mom has cluttered countertops, jam-packed closets, a nightmare of a basement, and a professional organizer for a daughter. Go figure.

Bottom Line: Keeping your client relationships professional will maximize your effectiveness, even though it might cost you some fun new friendships.

36/50   Assuming It's Obvious to Them

If you're naturally organized, here's some irony for ya: You might actually have a harder time teaching other people to be organized. Think about it. Some people in our industry were disorganized and figured out systems that worked to finally get their lives in order; now they teach those and other systems step by step to their clients. Others of us have been organized all our lives; we never needed to think about it step by step until starting an organizing business—it just came naturally. Growing up, we often didn't even realize we had this special ability: When praised for some innovative technique, we'd reply, "Well, duh, doesn't everybody do that?"

No duh about it, not everybody does what we do! Here are some of the things that caught me by surprise when I discovered they weren't intuitive to my clients:

Categorizing

Grouping items or data by category, based on their common function or some other similarity, is an epiphany for many clients. They've simply never thought of it. Most people use an alphabetical system for filing, but for many that's as far as they know how to go. Introducing the concept of grouping similar things together has revolutionized many a client's files, closets, task lists, drawers, and life.

Spatial Relations

This one took several years for me to notice, but now that I'm aware of it, it helps me home right in on the problem. I can simply look at an object and a space and know whether the object will fit into the space. Many of my clients can't do this, whether it's a box and a shelf, or a piece of furniture and an area in a room. When clients have empty shelves and stuff that needs to be put away, or when their furniture is arranged inefficiently, it usually turns out that they lack this ability to eyeball how things could fit. Sometimes they can't envision it even if they measure. This is not a deficit in intelligence—just a difference in how our brains process visual data. If you have this ability, use it for your clients who don't.

Putting Things Away

This sounds so basic, but often clients do need us to point out the cause-and-effect relationship between not putting things away and having clutter. Again, it's not that they're unintelligent; they just don't realize this connection as clearly as we do. Plus, a million things can interfere with putting things away, which explains how the efficiency industries of time management, productivity, and operational systems design became entwined with the spatial and aesthetic industries of object organization, decluttering, and interior decorating. We're bridging all of those worlds when we teach clients how to build habits that keep them and their spaces organized, and many of us are doing it intuitively, at least at first.

Bottom Line: Learn to identify the things you "just know" and find language and techniques to teach them to others who don't share your intuitive understanding.

37/50   Saying Inappropriate Things

You know better than to swear like a rap star when talking to clients (although when I greet their kids with "'sup?" I can actually get them to crack a smile). I'm not going to spend time on the obvious: politics, religion, sex, drugs. Let's consider some of the more subtle ways your words can get you into trouble:

Arguing

Sooner or later, we all encounter a "yeah but"-er. You know, a client whose response to everything is, "Yeah, but. . . ." It's frustrating and it can be really tough not to argue when you know you're right on at least some points. But don't. Arguing rarely leads to a meeting of the minds; you might get what you want for the moment, but they'll change it all back when you leave.

Scolding

Nobody wants to be scolded, and no one who is not your child should have to put up with it from you. Aim for positive rather than negative reinforcement with your clients.

Refereeing

Things really heat up when one spouse hires you and the other one thinks you're a waste of money and a poor solution to your client's laziness. Yikes! Talk like that makes me want to sit that insensitive oaf down for a sharp talking-to full of long words and attitude. But . . . deep breath . . . that's not our job. It's also not safe, for you or the client. Be supportive of the person you're there to help, but don't openly side with one family member against another, or with a worker against the boss. You must remain objective and keep a professional distance in order to be effective.

Confiding

Sharing personal information with a client can strengthen your working relationship, to a point. Telling a client a funny or disastrous story about a time you forgot a meeting can help them to see that no one is perfectly organized. Showing up for a session with a tear-stained face and a tale about your cheating mate is a big no-no. The client/professional relationship is not meant to be an even give-and-take: We help them with their problems, not the other way around.

Connecting on Social Media

Related to the previous point, allowing clients to connect with you on social media can have unintended negative consequences. These could be as benignly awkward as your client complimenting how you looked in that swimsuit, or as devastating as a client firing you because they disapprove of your politics, religion, or personal life choices. Be judicious with what you share in public vs. private posts and think carefully before allowing clients to connect with your personal accounts.

Bottom Line: Always remain mindful of what you say and how you say it when talking to clients and their significant others.

38/50   Giving In to Time Wasters

How many times a day do you check your email or social media accounts? At times it's like a nervous tic with me— whenever I'm frustrated, distracted, anxious, impatient, or generally not feeling good about whatever I'm working on at my desk, I start flipping through apps: email, Facebook, Twitter, Instagram. If there's nothing new, I might hit refresh just in case I missed something. I'm starting to think this is what it's like to have one of those morphine drips with a button you can push to dose yourself.

At least I had the sense to turn off audible notifications so they won't interrupt me when I am finally concentrating. But that still doesn't stop me from going in periodically and wasting some time wandering around in the inbox or newsfeeds. And invariably those feeds have ads or links, and before I know it, poof, it's an hour later and I'm about ten screens deep in some online store or blog.

What are your biggest time wasters? For some people it's phone calls (especially from friends who think working from home isn't work). For others, it's television, game apps, texting, or YouTube. Why are these things so appealing? If your time wasters are keeping you from work you know you should be doing, then they get another name: procrastination.

I think of clicking over to those apps as a form of "micro-procrastination." If I'm working on something frustrating and its completion is still far off, I find that I need to complete something, even something as inconsequential as checking my email, in order to feel a sense of accomplishment, short-lived as it is.

If you sometimes feel the need for micro-procrastination, start replacing email checks or a "quick" look at your socials with small tasks that actually do need to be done. When you work from home, this is very easy to do. Being careful not to get drawn away from work into more involved household projects, you might try these productive micro-procrastinations:

- loading the dishwasher
- filling pets' water bowls
- watering plants
- checking the postal mail
- taking out the trash

In an office setting, you could:

- walk to the supply cabinet for more Post-its
- refill your water bottle
- read an article in a business journal

No matter where you are, you could do a 30-second set of simple stretches or movements to get your blood flowing again (and yes, there are apps for that).

Tip: Don't let snacking become your time-waster or micro-procrastination of choice!

Bottom Line: Develop your awareness of how, and how often, you allow yourself to be distracted.

39/50   Handling Their Stuff
Disrespectfully

This is one that came to me naturally, and eventually I recognized that it goes a long way toward making my clients feel respected: It's the way in which I handle their belongings.

I call it using "Vanna Hands." You know, like Vanna White on *Wheel of Fortune,* or like any spokesmodel when they're handling a product. Instead of pointing at an object with one finger ("Do you want that?"), I gesture toward it with my entire hand, palm up ("Tell me about this item."). When I pick something up, even something that's about to be thrown away, I don't use just my thumb and one finger (the classic "eewwww" grip). I actually grip it, knowing that I'll wash my hands later. (If it's truly dirty, I find a rag or paper towel to line my hand.)

When holding an item for a client to consider, I hold it as if it's a prize someone is about to win: supported underneath by one hand and on one side by the other hand. (I find it so annoying to see Academy Award winners holding Oscar by his neck. . . .)

When the client decides to part with an item, instead of throwing it into a wastebasket or bag, I place it there. There is a world of difference in the impression you make throwing vs. placing a recently-parted-with former treasure. I do this even if the client seems neutral or unattached to the item.

One exception is when the client openly despises an item. If it's clear that they have bad feelings about the item and have been keeping it for the wrong reasons (guilt, misplaced loyalty, etc.), and if they then say something like, "My ex gave me that, and I've always hated that piece of crap—chuck it!" then it's appropriate to respond, "Well, heck yeah, out it goes!" and toss it with gusto. If it seems like the client wants to disrespect the item as a way of breaking emotional ties with it, follow their lead.

Note that "Vanna Hands" is more important with personal items like clothing, mementos, and dolls, stuffed animals, artwork, or anything else with a face than it is with papers, but no matter what, don't just fling stuff around.

Bottom Line: Your respect (or lack thereof) shows in your handling of clients' belongings, even their discards.

40/50   Not Developing Your Teaching Skills

Did you ever have a teacher who was obviously brilliant, knew their subject inside and out, but just could not make you understand it? If your work with clients involves not just putting their systems in place but also teaching them how to use and maintain those systems, you need to know more than just how to organize: You must also be able to explain organizing to someone who doesn't "get" it.

Practice on friends and family. (Ask for volunteers; don't just spring it on them spontaneously, as we naturally organized people are notorious for doing.) Keeping in mind that your personal relationship with them might make it more difficult for them to take you seriously or to really "hear" you, this is still a decent way to begin developing your teaching style.

You can also role-play on your own at home: Stand in front of one of your meticulously organized spaces, pretend there's someone there admiring it with you, and explain how you made it that way, step by step. Be especially careful not to skip over the most basic points, such as how you chose the size and shape of containers or why you put a particular item on a high shelf instead of a low one. You could even set up your phone and record yourself, then watch the recording the same way elite athletes watch their "post-games."

Once you're fairly comfortable with explaining spatial organization, challenge yourself to talk through processes for organizing data or time. It gets tougher as you progress from three-dimensional objects to the flattened realm of data and the fully symbolic realm of time.

As you practice, pay attention to your tone of voice. Do you sound excited to be conveying this information? Do you sound superior? Are you bragging? Imagine you're the student: Would you want to listen to you?

Bottom Line: If you love organizing, your clients will pick up on your enthusiasm. Find just the right words to make it all clear to them and you'll be their hero.

41/50   Spending Too Much on Overhead

Overhead means the expenses of running your business: the cost of your office's physical space (utility bills, rent, etc.), marketing, membership dues, and on and on. Let's admit it: It's kind of fun to have "business expenses"—it makes you sound important, and you get to spend money without guilt because "it's a write-off!"

Okay, back to reality. We PO/PCs are consultants, and a consulting business is very cost-effective to run. There's no need for a storefront or leased office space: You set up an email address and a business phone line or Google Voice number, and you work from home. Nowadays, you can do many of the tasks that businesses once had to outsource, such as printing business cards and brochures. You don't need warehouse space to stockpile a product.

All in all, consultants don't have a lot of overhead. So don't create overhead you don't need!

A local business associate once tried to persuade me to rent a portion of his office space. "C'mon Debbie, it'd be fun, we'd get to work in the same building! We could go to lunch all the time! And you'd have a snazzy office to impress your clients!"

I was tempted, for a minute. Yes, it would be nice to have other people around instead of toiling away in isolation when I'm doing office work. And yes, it would be an ego boost to have a fancy address and an actual office outside of my home. But the reality is that I can go out to lunch with a friend or colleague whenever I want, and I see my clients mostly virtually and once in a while in their homes and offices. It wouldn't make sense for them to come to me. In the end I realized it just wasn't right for my type of business (and he probably just wanted someone else to help with the rent).

If you simply must spend some money in a I'm-a-business-owner kind of way, sign up as a named sponsor for a charitable event. You might even get some client leads out of it.

Bottom Line: Don't buy stuff your business doesn't need.

42/50   Ignoring Your Past Expertise

When PO/PCs get to talking, one of the first questions is usually, "What did you do before this?" Whether you were a teacher, office manager, homemaker, police officer, accountant, attorney, therapist, student, or (this was an interesting one) asbestos expert, the skills and knowledge you acquired before becoming a PO/PC can come back to serve you in your client work.

My career before this was in publishing. I've worked as a newspaper reporter, photographer, and reference book editor, so I have strong editorial skills that I can use to help other PO/PCs and my clients with their writing projects, from resumes to books of their own.

I also have a background in martial arts: I've studied in several different styles and have taught self-defense for many years, so my knowledge of personal safety helps me to be safe with visits to strangers' homes and businesses, and I pass that expertise on to my peers with courses on safety for onsite consultants and my book *"Let Me Show You the Basement": A Guide to Staying Safe in Clients' Homes.*

How can you merge your "past life" with your new one as a PO/PC? What special interests or hobbies do you enjoy that could provide valuable insight for your clients?

Often when people go into business for themselves, they want to start fresh with something completely different from the job they just left behind. If this is you, explore some organizing specialties that are interesting, even if they're alien to you.

Eventually, though (after you get past that feeling of "thank goodness I never have to do *that* again!"), the work you did before might find its way into the work you're doing now. Chances are it will make you an even better PO/PC.

Your past skills can also come back into service if you hit a slump in business, or you can use your self-employed freedom to try out some other part-time work that you wouldn't have needed or had time for with a traditional full-time job. In the modern gig economy, you can easily add a job unrelated to your career (like dogs? Sign up with a dog-walking app) and work only as much as you want to. There's no shame in supplementing your PO/PC income with other work as needed.

Bottom Line: Drawing on your past expertise can help you to find your ideal place in the world of professional organizing and productivity.

43/50   Neglecting Your Personal Life

Ring, ring!

"Hey!"

"Hey Deb, whatcha doin'?"

"Workin'"

There it is: the story of my life in the early years of self-employment. Whenever a friend called, they'd almost always catch me at my desk doing something work-related.

Nowadays, it's not that bad. I do work a lot (a *lot,* I tell you), but it's been worse. When I started my company, I was obsessed with making it successful. My eyes flew open in the morning and I went straight to my desk: Check the email! Check the voicemail! Write that article! Read that book!

On days I had client appointments, I'd stop the deskwork long enough to get ready and go, then would come straight back and resume my never-ending administrative tasks. I was so focused, I didn't even take time to shop in actual stores: I ordered clothes from catalogs, and it didn't fully register that I was needing bigger and bigger sizes. . . .

After a couple of frenetic years, I decided I had to carve out time for myself. The thing I most wanted to do was make time for exercise, but I simply could not force myself to take time to go to a gym or to work out before starting my day. I couldn't wait to get to work!

My solution was to hire a personal trainer to come to my home three days a week, drag me away from my desk, and make me work out. It took a full six months of that before I stopped longing for the computer mouse instead of hand weights, before I could spend 45 minutes on the treadmill without freaking out if the work phone rang, and before I actually started to enjoy exercise again.

Now I'm self-sufficient with fitness, and over time I've progressively learned a lot about nutrition and refined my eating habits, operating within the perspective of food as a tool, not a toy. I make a conscious effort to socialize with friends, although sometimes I have to force myself not to think about the work waiting to be done. And I'm trying not to neglect sleep in favor of work. (That will be a lifelong battle, I'm sure.)

If you recognize yourself in this story, bring more balance into your life before you burn out. You need downtime to replenish your creativity and rebuild your energy so you can give 100% when you are working. This is not just encouragement; it's neuroscience.

If your business is still in the building stage, be a workaholic for now if you must, but set a deadline by which you promise yourself that you'll transition to a more manageable lifestyle.

Bottom Line: Business success will be bittersweet if the rest of your life falls apart.

44/50   Nursing a Fear of Public Speaking

I am eternally grateful that nothing bad happened to me in high school speech class, because that seems to be where many public-speaking phobias are born. I know how fortunate I am to have escaped this very common fear.

I've known colleagues to devote hours to preparing to speak at an event for which I spent 15 minutes dashing off a few notes, and we both did just fine, although the colleague was an emotional wreck by the end. We've all seen someone break into a sweat when called upon to make some impromptu remarks.

I watch nervous speakers and think it must be awful to struggle like that, and every time, I give thanks once again for my freedom from this terror. (By the way, I did get stuck with a bona fide phobia in life, but it's wasps—not nearly as debilitating in business as the fear of speaking.)

If you share the fear of public speaking, you're in good and plentiful company. Nonetheless, it's in your best interest to work past it. PO/PCs are frequently called upon to speak to community groups, to give workshops for their peers, and, scariest of all, to be interviewed in the press or appear on radio or television touting the glories of getting organized. If you're not able to do these things, you will miss out on many opportunities to promote your business and gain new clients.

There are many books out there about learning to be an

engaging, impactful speaker. Articles are written about it all the time, full of tips on getting over your anxiety. Who hasn't heard that classic line, "Picture the audience naked"?

However, from what I've seen of people who have overcome this fear, the thing that works best is practice, and a great option for practice is Toastmasters International, a membership organization with over 16,000 chapters in 145 countries. Its education program helps members to become more effective in every aspect of public speaking (not just giving toasts).

Go to the Toastmasters website to find the clubs closest to you and visit a few of them. Some meet at lunchtime during the week and are focused on members from the business world; others meet in the evening and have members of various backgrounds. The atmosphere is supportive, with the emphasis on giving and receiving constructive feedback and honing your skills in a safe environment.

Bottom Line: Grow your business by outgrowing your fear of public speaking.

45/50   Trusting Others to Be Ethical

If you're an ethical person, you might tend to expect the same from others. I prefer to think the best of people and usually I'm not disappointed. Still, I've learned firsthand that in business, as in life, there will always be people who are out to take you for whatever they can. The difference in business is that it's often more costly.

So watch out for the con artists. Don't be shy about asking for written details or guarantees. If you're uncomfortable telling someone you don't trust their word, insist that you want a written agreement to make sure *they* feel they can trust *you*, and don't back down.

Or better yet, don't do business with someone who gives you an "uh-oh" feeling. Before you trust someone, ask yourself what's in it for them. Are they really being nice to you just to be nice, or do you have something they want? Figure out the other person's motivation and you'll have a head start toward knowing how much to trust them.

Trust your intuition: If it's telling you it's a scam, it probably is.

Even in situations fraught with suspicion and negativity, don't allow your optimism to be replaced with cynicism. There's no need to be wary of everyone if you take reasonable precautions against being swindled by unethical people.

Ethics matter in our own business practices as well. I believe that people often don't realize they're doing something unethical, or they realize it only in hindsight. Educating yourself about ethical theory and risk avoidance can help prevent inadvertent lapses.

This is a topic I developed an especially strong interest in while completing my counseling degree, so I wrote several courses and a book on ethics for PO/PCs to continue growing my own knowledge and to help others avoid ethical pitfalls. If you want a deeper dive into ethical theory, check out my book *Ethical Pitfalls for Professional Organizers* and my NAPO course "Ethics and Policies for Working with Clients with Brain-based Conditions."

Bottom Line: Trust others, but trust your intuition equally if not more.

46/50   Waiting for the Phone to Ring

They say good things come to those who wait. I don't know who "they" are, but they don't know much about increasing one's client base!

You have two choices for finding clients: the passive approach and the proactive approach. If you want to work a lot, you need to be proactive. If you want just a little bit of business as you get started or you only want to work part-time, passive is the way to go.

The passive approach to finding clients is waiting for them to come to you through whatever means you've used to publicize your services (your website, your social media accounts, the member directories of professional groups you've joined) or perhaps via word of mouth from friends, family, and past clients.

A proactive approach to acquiring clients includes options such as:

- purchasing advertising
- teaching classes on getting organized
- enacting an intentional social media marketing strategy
- contacting local groups who need speakers for their meetings
- submitting press releases to local papers and TV news shows
- partnering with a retail provider of organizing supplies
- joining business networking groups

- setting up a referral-sharing system with other companies in your area that serve the same demographic of clients

Doing just one of these things is likely to bring you at least one new client; do all of them and you're bound to get busy real quick!

Bottom Line: If you can only handle a small amount of business, wait for clients to come to you. If your company is in aggressive-growth mode, take a proactive approach to acquiring clients.

47/50   Letting Yourself Be "Gifted"

Lots of businesses sell gift certificates for their services or products. You can too . . . if you still want to after reading this pitfall.

The very big problem with gift certificates and also with being hired by one person to work with another is when the recipient doesn't want you. Often, what's really going on here is that the PO/PC's service is something the giver thinks the recipient needs, whether or not the recipient agrees with that assessment or is ready to do anything about it.

We've all had the experience of receiving a gift that was really all about the giver: The hand-crocheted kitchen towels that don't match your décor, but which you're supposed to appreciate because your mother-in-law worked so hard on them; the fancy rotisserie that you can now use to make "better" meals for your family; the treadmill that you look like you nee-, er, that I thought you said you wanted. . . .

Imagine how you would feel if someone gifted you with an image consultant or gym membership or plastic surgeon, and you had not requested it? How about inferior, underappreciated, judged, humiliated, and ambushed? That's how people we're "given" to often feel.

This doesn't mean you can't offer gift certificates for your services. Just make absolutely sure that the recipient does want the gift and will cooperate with you. If the gift is a surprise, meaning you're unable to talk to the recipient beforehand, grill the buyer for clues that the gift might not be as welcomed as they seem to believe.

In a business setting it can be even stickier: If a supervisor wants to hire you to "fix" an employee, think very carefully before accepting the job. Insist on talking to the employee first, and if you sense that the employee is hostile to the idea, respectfully decline the job: Chances are slim to none that that situation would turn out well for either of you.

Important: NEVER participate in tricking someone into leaving so you can purge their stuff. It causes profound emotional trauma. In some cases, the person being "helped" has become suicidal. Plus, you could be charged with burglary. If someone asks you to help clear out Mom's apartment while she's gone for the weekend, say no and do everything you can to talk them out of it!

Bottom Line: If you offer gift certificates, put policies in place to keep the offering safe for the recipient.

48/50   Not Seeing the Forest for the Trees

I mean this one both in your client work and in running your business. There are many times when we, both as PO/PCs and as business owners, are called upon to see the big picture and the details at the same time.

In helping a client to declutter a room, apply order to paperwork, plan an event, or adopt a better approach to time management, we examine many small components—each object, space, document, task, and appointment—while considering how each of those components interacts with the others and how they all come together to make up the end result the client desires. That's a lot to keep in your head.

The same is true of keeping your business operating at peak efficiency. You have to watch each dollar you earn and spend, and manage every one of your days, sometimes minute by minute, while never losing sight of your annual budget and your long-term business plan. It is so very easy to get caught up in the grind of answering emails and phone calls, squeezing clients into every available time slot, and fitting in personal obligations. No wonder it can seem like we blink and it's already a new year.

Think about which you're better at: big picture or details, the forest or the trees. Then schedule regular appointments with yourself to practice the one that needs work.

If it's the forest, force yourself to spend at least a half-hour each week thinking about your company's future. Even if you reach no conclusions, get into the habit of periodically focusing on next week, next month, next year—anything but right-this-minute. After a while it will start to pay off in the form of a more global perspective.

If it's the trees that elude you, you get to have some fun: Take a few minutes each day to play a computer or phone game that rewards you for attention to detail. Work crossword puzzles to practice accurately seeing something through to completion. Play "I Spy" with yourself when you're out for a walk: How many yellow doors or blue birds or purple flowers do you see? Do word-search puzzles (or real puzzles!) to train your eye to find the items you want amid the unneeded ones—in other words, amid clutter!

Tip: Help your clients with their forests and trees too. Offer them these exercises or devise some of your own.

Bottom Line: We need to be adept with both the micro and the macro view.

49/50   Tolerating Bias

There's this scene from a movie that I think of every time I hear evidence of a biased attitude regarding me, my business, or one of my clients. In the scene, a mean girl says something cruel to a nice girl. The nice girl's boyfriend steps up to the meanie and, wagging a finger in her face, says, "Uh-uh. Not cool."

I feel like doing that every time a female client's husband says, "So, you go around cleaning up after housewives, huh?" or when a client's family member says, "How can you stand to spend every day with these ADD people? We can barely tolerate living with just one!" or when an older businessperson takes a condescending tone with me and says, "Oh, you own your own business? How cute! Is it that one where you sell makeup door to door, or the one where you sell candles at parties?"

Obviously, I can't make a habit of correcting every ignorant and insensitive remark I hear. But I do take every opportunity to educate when I think it's possible to change the speaker's mind and/or when my reputation or my client's self-esteem is at stake.

The trick to standing up to biased attitudes is reacting as if you believe the speaker had no intention of offending and would want you to offer discreet enlightenment. Even if you're thinking, "What a jerk!," you can respond diplomatically, non-confrontationally, and once in a while you'll actually change how they think.

For the judgmental husband, I might say (in a light tone even though inside I'm seething), "Actually, I work with business as well as residential clients." If he takes the bait and says, "Oh, you work with businesspeople too?" I'll say, "I sure do, and actually, that's easier because they tend to have fewer responsibilities than homemakers."

For the family of the client with AD/HD, I might respond (again, lightly), "Actually I love working with people with ADD. They tend to be smarter than the average person, friendlier, more creative . . . they just need a little coaching in being organized."

With that businessperson intent on treating me like a child, I'd say something like, "I don't sell product. I'm a productivity consultant for corporations and small businesses, and I also offer individual coaching. I'd be happy to take your card if you're interested in sharing referrals."

Bottom Line: The best way to combat biases is by conducting business in a way that disproves them.

50/50   Not Knowing the Value of Your Time

Let's wrap up our 50 pitfalls with one that will serve you very well for the rest of your career, and the rest of your life.

As PO/PCs, we tend to know better than most people that it's impossible to do everything. Still, it's sobering to reach that point where you realize that, in order to do one thing, you're going to have to say no to five others.

If you bill for your services by the hour, you'll have a head start toward avoiding this pitfall. Once you become accustomed to clients paying you a certain amount per hour for your time, you'll start to think of other hours, like those spent sitting in a waiting room or languishing on hold, as not just a waste of time, but a quantifiable waste of money.

Get into the habit of asking yourself whether it's worth doing. And what is "it"? Anything that takes time (i.e. everything). Not all time spent needs to be productive (sometimes doing nothing for a while is the healthiest choice) but as a self-employed person, I'd bet you're more likely to "waste" time actively, on things that appear to be productive but actually aren't. Are these worth it?

- Driving 15 minutes out of your way to use a gas station that charges 7 cents per gallon less than the others.
- Standing in line at a store for 10 minutes to return an item that cost $5.

- Spending an hour browsing through eBay just to see what's there.
- Spending hours going through the Small Claims Court process to recoup $100 from a client who didn't pay. (Don't tell me it's the principle of the thing; if someone did you wrong, why compound it by wasting more of your time and money on a vendetta?)

Once you've gotten good at this, you'll see a bonus payoff: You will serve as an even better example to your clients. People are accustomed to thinking that they should save money any way they can, no matter how much time it takes and no matter how little money it is. This, of course, is one of the main causes of clutter!

For my clients, clutter control and time management are intertwined, because I ask them again and again, "Is caring for this item worth the expense of your time?" This perspective makes it much easier for them to weed out unworthy items (in their closets and in their schedules) and give more attention to the important ones.

Assign a dollar value to an hour of your time, then think about what each step in your daily routine "costs" you. You'll soon find yourself better respecting your own time and helping clients to respect theirs as well.

Bottom Line: Spend your time as wisely as you spend your money.

About the Author

Debbie Stanley, MA, MS, LPC, is a licensed mental health counselor, organizational psychologist, author, speaker, and president of Thoughts in Order Counseling and Consulting, founded in 1997 in metro Detroit and now based in Austin, TX.

She is a member of the National Association of Productivity & Organizing Professionals (NAPO) and NAPO-Austin, a member and past president of NAPO-Michigan, a recipient of NAPO's Founder's Award and Shining Star Award, and a founding board member of the Institute for Challenging Disorganization.

Beyond the organizing and productivity industry, Debbie is co-founder of the nonprofit Austin Music Export and a professional member of the National Academy of Recording Arts and Sciences.

Debbie works with clients individually and in groups, specializing in chronic disorganization and the music industry, and offers peer consultation. She is also a frequent guest speaker and presenter of workshops and conference sessions.

Learn more at ThoughtsInOrder.com

Resources by Debbie Stanley

Courses for PO/PCs available on demand at napo.net

- "Ethics and Policies for Working with Clients with Brain-based Conditions"
- "Fundamental Organizing and Productivity Principles"
- "Safety in the Organizing Environment"

Books for PO/PCs available at Amazon.com

- *Ethical Pitfalls for Professional Organizers*
- *"Let Me Show You the Basement": A Guide to Staying Safe in Clients' Homes*
- *Newbie Pitfalls: 50 Obstacles to Success as a Professional Organizer and How to Avoid Them*

Books for clients available at Amazon.com

- *Organize Your Home in No Time*
- *The Organized Musician*